WHITE FUNNEL
PADDLE STEAMERS
In the Bristol Channel

**Compiled by Mike Tedstone from the archives of
the Paddle Steamer Preservation Society**

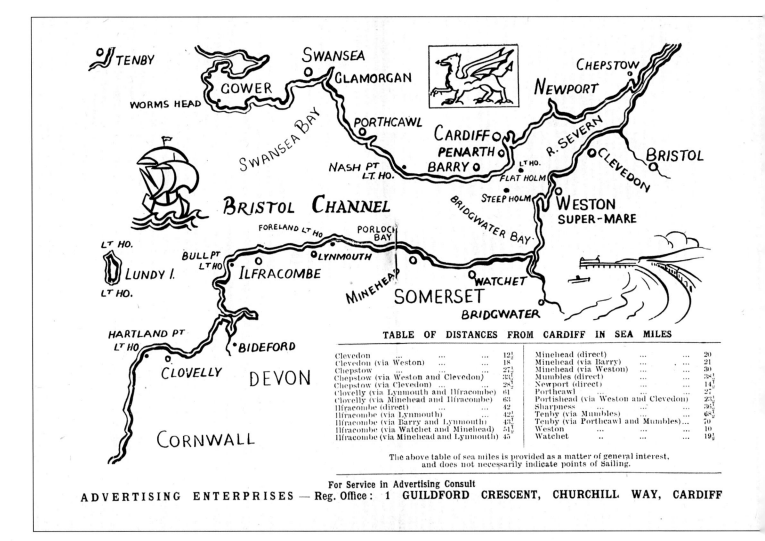

TABLE OF DISTANCES FROM CARDIFF IN SEA MILES

Clevedon	...	...	...	12½
Clevedon (via Weston)	...	...	...	18
Chepstow	...	...	...	27½
Chepstow (via Weston and Clevedon)	...	...	33½	
Chepstow (via Clevedon)	...	...	...	28½
Clovelly (via Lynmouth and Ilfracombe)	61			
Clovelly (via Minehead and Ilfracombe)	63			
Ilfracombe (direct)	...	...	...	42
Ilfracombe (via Lynmouth)	...	...	42½	
Ilfracombe (via Barry and Lynmouth)	...	43½		
Ilfracombe (via Watchet and Minehead)	...	51½		
Ilfracombe (via Minehead and Lynmouth)	45			
Minehead (direct)	...	...	...	20
Minehead (via Barry)	...	...	...	21
Minehead (via Weston)	...	...	30	
Mumbles (direct)	...	...	...	38½
Newport (direct)	...	...	...	14½
Porthcawl	...	...	...	27
Portishead (via Weston and Clevedon)	...	23½		
Sharpness	...	...	...	36½
Tenby (via Mumbles)	...	...	68½	
Tenby (via Porthcawl and Mumbles)	...	70		
Weston	...	...	...	10
Watchet	...	...	...	19½

The above table of sea miles is provided as a matter of general interest,
and does not necessarily indicate points of Sailing.

Published by Mainline & Maritime Ltd, 3 Broadleaze, Upper Seagry, near Chippenham, SN15 5EY
Tel: 07770 748615 www.mainlineandmaritime.co.uk orders@mainlineandmaritime.co.uk
Printed in the UK

ISBN: 978-1-913797-09-6 © Mainline & Maritime Ltd, Paddle Steamer Preservation Society & Author 2022

Front Cover: A classic postcard view of the Clifton Suspension Bridge spanning the Avon Gorge. The locally built paddle steamer *Bristol Queen* of 1946, having left the Hotwells Pontoon a few minutes earlier, is setting off for a cruise down the Bristol Channel.

Frontispiece: *Bristol Queen* at Clovelly beach.

Back Cover: The Clyde-built paddle steamer *Cardiff Queen*, built in 1947, and thus a close relative of the celebrated *Waverley*, the last seagoing paddle steamer in the world, lies alongside Ilfracombe Pier on 23 September 1961. *Cardiff Queen* lasted until just 1966; a tragically short life.

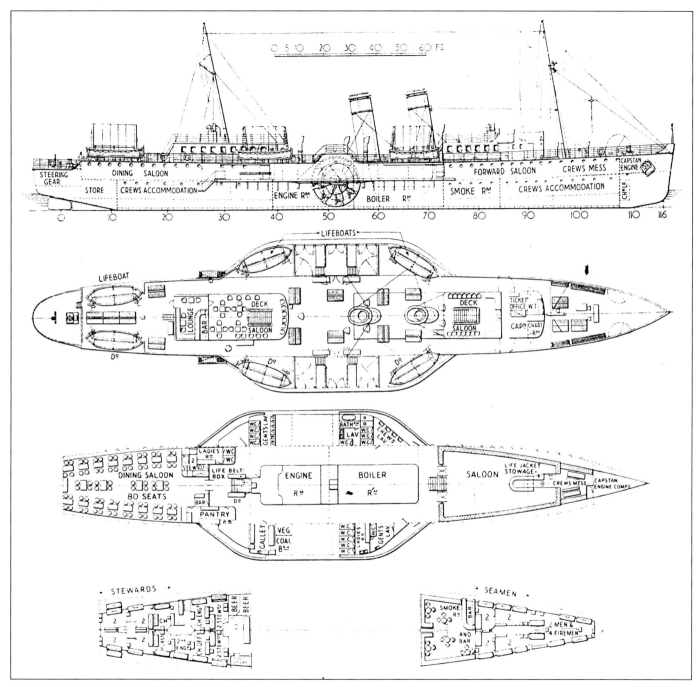

The General Arrangement (GA) of the Bristol-built, ps ***Bristol Queen*** of 1946. To modern-day members of the PSPS, familiar with the layout of near-contemporary ***Waverley***, ordered by the LNER, there are extensive similarities in layout, if not exactly style. Apart from sharing the same supplier of engines, Rankin & Blackmore, and possessing two funnels, and forward and aft deckhouse structures, and of comparable length, perhaps the most stark difference is that the LNER ship featured an enclosed deckhouse, whereas the Bristol ship had an open bridge. The Purser's office is perhaps the other main difference, along with the galley location.

INTRODUCTION

Origins & Early History

Bristol had been the headquarters of P. & A. Campbell Ltd, since 1888 when the brothers Peter and Alexander (Alec) Campbell introduced the first **Waverley** (built in 1885 for Clyde service) on the Ilfracombe run from the city. Their venture proved such a success that in 1891 they introduced the purpose-built **Ravenswood** and over the next few years added the famous "fliers" **Westward Ho**, **Cambria** and **Britannia** together with several second hand vessels.

The White Funnel Fleet reached its greatest strength of fourteen ships in the years immediately prior to the First World War. Three - **Devonia**, **Barry** and **Tintern** (ex **Westonia**) - had been taken over from the rival 'Red Funnel' Barry fleet, the brand-new **Glen Avon** and **Glen Usk** had been added and the veteran **Bonnie Doon** disposed of.

Two of the fleet were lost to enemy action during the First World War and three more were subsequently scrapped as unfit for reconditioning. These were replaced by some second-hand acquisitions and just one new ship, the **Glen Gower** (b.1922), which was fitted with engines taken from the **Albion** (b.1893) when she had been broken up. During the inter-war years White Funnel Fleet strength typically remained at eleven vessels, all paddle steamers.

The Postwar Fleet

The Second World War saw a further five steamers lost and two more rendered beyond economical repair. Only four paddle steamers survived the conflict in sufficiently good order to be refitted for further service. The two oldest survivors, **Ravenswood** (b.1891) and **Britannia** (b.1896) required extensive reconstruction which considerably altered their appearance. Although modernised, they were still of a distinctly venerable character when Norman Bird travelled on and began to photograph them in earnest during the early 1950s. The other pair of survivors were the newer **Glen Usk** (b.1914) and **Glen Gower** (b.1922). This quartet of paddle steamers still had plenty of life left in them as services gradually got going again in 1946-47. They were joined during 1946 and 1947 by the splendid newly-built, modern steamers **Bristol Queen** and **Cardiff Queen**. Campbell's post-war fleet therefore represented a fascinating cross section of steamer design, from the Victorian to the most contemporary. The fleet remained stable until 1955 when a period of steady contraction began. **Ravenswood** was first to go, followed over the next eight years by the three other "veterans" so that, by 1963 only the **Cardiff Queen** and **Bristol Queen** remained. Victims of changing fashion and policy, rising costs and poor maintenance these too were withdrawn in 1966 and 1967 respectively.

THE WHITE FUNNEL FLEET

Steamer	Length		Beam		Shaft H.P.
	Ft.	ins.	Ft.	ins.	
T.S.S. EMPRESS QUEEN	269	6	37	6	4194
P.S. BRISTOL QUEEN	244	8½	31	0	Indicated H.P. 2500
P.S. CARDIFF QUEEN	240	0	30	0	2200
P.S. BRITANNIA	230	0	26	6	2400
P.S. GLEN USK	224	3	28	1	1500
P.S. GLEN GOWER	235	1	28	5	1500
P.S. RAVENSWOOD	215	0	24	1	1200

The Territory

Together these six paddle steamers enabled postwar excursions to be operated from four principal starting-points, namely Bristol, Newport, Cardiff and Swansea in addition to Barry Pier which, with its rail access, played an important role in putting additional passengers on board the vessels of the White Funnel Fleet.

At its postwar peak in the mid-1950s, the territory sailed by the six paddle steamers was just as extensive as it had been in the heyday before the Great War when the fleet was twice the size. A typical full day out from Cardiff to Clovelly might easily occupy 12 or 13 hours, but the well-found ships were built for such voyages, and demand was seemingly still as strong as ever. A great array of delightful destinations was available, with the excitement of epic scenery on the way, whether cruising past the high North Devon coastal cliffs, out to Lundy Island, or around Gower Peninsula and across Carmarthen Bay. Even after 1954 when the fleet began gradually to contract, most routes continued to operate and it is during the latter part of the decade that most of the photographs in this compilation were taken. They illustrate the huge variety of trips which Norman Bird undertook in all members of the fleet and to virtually everywhere on the map, including some rarely visited destinations such as far flung Padstow, which Campbells "rediscovered" during the 1960s.

The Photographs

Rather than proceed chronologically, I have begun the album by looking closely at each of the four "veterans", classically posed at sea. All were impressive and smartly kept, but each was subtly different and had a character of her own. Enthusiasts could take delight in minute details, and appreciate how paddle steamer design had evolved from the 1890s. Norman did not flinch from photographing each of them as they finally departed, under tow, to be broken up after their withdrawal, and a number of those "final moments" images are included.

The remainder of the book consists of images of practically all the piers and harbours which the steamers visited around the English and Welsh sides of the Bristol Channel. This tour of the Bristol Channel as a White Funnel Fleet paddle steamer enthusiast would have enjoyed it, begins at Bristol and continues down the Avon Gorge, then along the English side of the Severn estuary to north Devon, before heading to Cornwall, and then Lundy. We then work our way back up the Welsh side of the Bristol Channel from Milford Haven in west Wales ending at the Severn Bridge, the opening of which in 1966 loosely coincided with the end of the paddle steamer era. It is quite clear, from what Norman Bird recorded, that he literally went everywhere it was then possible to go when the postwar territory was at its greatest extent, as a dedicated supporter of the White Funnel Fleet, but by the sixties we see only the more modern surviving **Bristol Queen** and **Cardiff Queen**.

The negatives from which these splendid photographs were printed came to light while a particularly large and important bequest to the Paddle Steamer Preservation Society Archive was being catalogued. The collection belonged to the late Chris Collard, a respected and prolific writer on Bristol Channel paddle steamers. They were discovered in a disintegrating shoe box containing an assortment of ephemera. Each negative, cut from 120 roll-film, was in an individual protective sleeve carefully labelled, dated and located in the distinctive hand writing of the late Norman Bird, and it quickly became apparent that they were of considerable historical value.

The PSPS has a large and growing archive containing over 50,000 items and aims to acquire, preserve, exhibit and publish as much as possible in order to educate the public in the significance of paddle steamers in the nation's maritime and industrial history. It was obvious that the newly discovered negatives were of such importance that they should be scanned for conservation and future use in digital form.

While that was taking place PSPS members were also preoccupied with fulfilling their other key aim, to maintain their two steamers **Waverley** and **Kingswear Castle** in sailing condition. The Covid 19 pandemic had severely disrupted their normal 2020 public sailing programmes and earning ability, so all thoughts were turned to raising sufficient funds to pay for future maintenance and refits.

It was in that context that the idea of this book arose. Through my interest in narrow gauge railways, I had become aware of Mainline & Maritime's Covid Fundraiser book publishing initiative and approached them to ask if they would consider publishing this book on behalf of the PSPS Bristol Channel Branch in support of **Waverley** and **Kingswear Castle**. To our delight they agreed, and PSPS would like to record its sincere thanks to Iain McCall for his support, which will ensure that £5 for every book sold will go directly to helping these two gems of Britain's maritime heritage sail on into the future.

Mike Tedstone
Purton, Wiltshire, April 2022

Above: A little of the atmosphere of the nineteen-fifties on an excursion steamer is evoked by this image used by P. & A. Campbell Ltd. of Bristol to encourage people to travel by sea on one of their seven-strong postwar fleet of White Funnel pleasure steamers – six paddle steamers, and the turbine-steamer Empress Queen.

THE PHOTOGRAPHER - NORMAN BIRD
27th March 1932 – 27th February 2018

The superb black and white photographs which form this book were all taken during the 1950s and early 1960s by the late Norman Bird, a sensitive, thoughtful and multi-talented man who, throughout his life, loved nothing better than to be afloat. Preferably on board a P. & A. Campbell Ltd. paddle steamer and, better still, on a windy day with a big sea running.

Norman was born and brought up in Cardiff where, before the Second World War, he first became aware of the distinctive white funnels of the Campbell steamers towering over the Pier Head pontoon at the bottom of Bute Street. On 16th April 1946, having scraped together the 1/6d fare, he made his first ever sailing, a single trip from Cardiff to Newport on board the veteran *Ravenswood*. He declared himself "hooked", and eagerly followed the return of the fleet to post-war service. News having already reached his ears that Campbells were building a new flagship to be named **Bristol Queen**, two pivotal moments came during September 1946 when he first glimpsed her running trials off Barry and, a few days later was on board for her maiden sailing from Cardiff to Ilfracombe. He was smitten and for the rest of his life **Bristol Queen** remained his favourite ship.

Norman did well at school but his parents could not afford to fund his further education so, as soon as he had completed his School Certificate, he obtained employment in Cardiff City Council's Finance Department. To those who knew his artistic and creative character this may have seemed an unlikely career, but doubtless the highly professional, meticulous approach he applied to everything he undertook would have made him an ideal employee. Initially his wages were quite low, so he was only able to afford a dozen or so steamer trips each season, but he made the most of these by sampling all of the Campbell steamers - **Ravenswood**, **Britannia**, **Glen Usk**, **Glen Gower**, **Cardiff Queen** and **Bristol Queen** - and even travelled to Brighton to sail in their splendid turbine screw steamer **Empress Queen**. He also fell in love with Lundy and, over the next half century was to visit the island as often as he was able.

By 1954 his financial position was much improved and henceforth his number of sailings rose to between 40 and 50 each season. His interest deepened, he struck up many lasting friendships with other enthusiasts who shared his passion, and became a founder member of the short-lived White Funnel Fleet Supporters' Association. Within a year that group's newsletter had transformed itself into *Ship Ahoy* the highly regarded quarterly journal of the South Wales Branch of the World Ship Society. Norman was a regular contributor and the views he expressed were often controversial. Whilst always acknowledging the things that P. & A. Campbell Ltd. did well, he was also happy to express strong and closely reasoned criticisms of their perceived failings! He recognised that the gradual disposal of the pre-war veteran steamers was inevitable, but was particularly exercised by

the spiral of falling revenue and poor maintenance which led to the premature demise of his beloved **Bristol Queen** during 1967. During 1968 and 1969 *Ship Ahoy* published Norman's superb, seven-part valedictory account of **Bristol Queen**'s career which mixed definitive year by year details with his lyrically expressed feelings about the ship. Many steamer historians still regard it as a classic piece of writing and are grateful to him for setting such a high standard to aspire to. When I began to undertake detailed research myself, I was always grateful for his perceptive but supportive probing, and knew that if anything I wrote passed "the Norman test" it was certain to be both grammatically and factually correct.

In 1961 Norman moved to Southampton to take up a new post at the Civic Centre, where he developed new skills in the then novel and arcane art of computer programming for financial control. He continued to visit the Bristol Channel whenever he could, revelling especially in long and unusual trips, but also took full advantage of the new opportunities available to him on the South Coast. These included Red Funnel's car ferries and their motor ships **Balmoral** and **Vecta**; the Portsmouth - Ryde passenger ships; Cosens' paddlers **Embassy** and **Consul** and a range of smaller vessels and cross channel ferries. He was an active member of the Paddle Steamer Preservation Society and Southampton Branch of the World Ship Society and was a great supporter of charter sailings organised by the two organisations.

I first met Norman in 1963 on board the **Princess Elizabeth** during a sailing from Weymouth. At that time, I was a bright eyed, 12 years old, junior member of the PSPS and perhaps Norman recognised something of his own youthful enthusiasm in me. In the years that followed he went out of his way to encourage my interest sending long, handwritten, informative letters and often including copies of his wonderful photographs. These were instantly recognisable as they were always printed without white borders on high gloss, double weight paper, and absolutely sparkled. He was a frequent visitor to Weymouth in order to sail on board **Consul** and **Princess Elizabeth** during their final years, we shared memorable trips on **Sandown** and **Ryde**, and I would sometimes visit him in Southampton for a return crossing to the Isle of Wight. On one occasion he arranged for us to go out on a Red Funnel tug to join the inward bound liner **Rotterdam** for a trip up Southampton Water, and I shall never forget the drenching we received on board the **Queen of the Isles** during a wet and windy trip from Weymouth on 15th September 1968 during her "round the land" positioning voyage from Barry to Dover. In the decades that followed we would bump into each other in many different locations around the coast and it became tradition with my wife and I, when waiting on one pier head or another, to scan the decks of the approaching steamer in the certain knowledge that, if Norman was on board, he would be spotted standing in his favourite spot right in the bows of the ship.

Norman did not limit his adventures to the South Coast and Bristol Channel, but travelled widely within Britain and abroad, sailing on interesting vessels wherever he could find them. Norway, Sweden, the Baltic and North Sea coasts of Germany, Sardinia, Corsica, Switzerland, Greece, Australia were all within his orbit, but he held an especially deep affection for the Bay of Naples, which he visited many times. He spent countless hours on board the local passenger ships, visiting Capri and the other islands and experiencing every possible route. His favourite ship was the veteran *Santa Maria del Mare*, which probably came second in his affections only to the *Bristol Queen*, and he spent many years researching the history of the local fleet. When travelling he loved to absorb himself deeply in the local landscape, architecture, culture, faiths and cuisine, and went out of his way to learn and use as much of the region's language as possible.

Indeed, his interests were wide ranging. He was a superb and adventurous cook, employing recipes from all around the world. He loved the arts, was a regular theatre-goer and had an eclectic taste in music. He was a connoisseur of opera and had a great love for the divas Maria Callas, Marlene Dietrich and, more than any other, Carmen Miranda. He had a good baritone voice and it was not unknown for him to break into song on the deck of an excursion steamer. The purser of the *Bristol Queen* was a fellow opera lover who would sometimes sing snatches of Verdi from the ticket office window and, on one notable occasion, delighted Norman by replacing the usual light music broadcast over the ship's loudspeakers with Wagner's "The Mastersingers of Nuremberg"… until other passengers complained! In the early 1950s he also won a number of medals for ballroom dancing.

Norman was tall, distinguished and in middle age sported a full, dark beard. He bore a distinct resemblance to Clement Freud, a fact that caused him mild annoyance and, on one memorable day when he was twice asked for his autograph, a distinct tetchiness! As he grew older his dress sense became ever more colourful, with the tweed jackets of the 1960s giving way to stylish but casual clothes in a range of vivid hues. He had dark, penetrating eyes which would blaze or twinkle in equal measure, a wonderful, sonorous Welsh accent and an extremely dry wit. He was an eloquent speaker with a fine command of both language and facts, and to witness him in full flow on any subject which interested him was a memorable pleasure.

He cared deeply about his family and friends and had a keen social conscience, so it was no surprise that in 1971 he decided to give up his career in computing, move to London and retrain as a social worker. He spent the next 16 years working in this highly demanding role for Westminster City Council before recognising his calling – which had been growing gradually louder over the past 25 years – to enter the Anglican Priesthood. Following his theological training, part of which took place in the West Indies, he was ordained priest in 1990 and went on to serve at two parishes in Willesden Green and Wembley. After 1998 when a combination of complex medical conditions forced him to retire from full time ministry, he retained his Permission to Officiate and provided welcome support to a number of local churches.

During his time in London Norman made many trips on the Thames, getting to know the passenger boats and their owners on trips up river to Hampton Court or down to the Thames Barrier. He only wanted to sail on boats with open decks, particularly the older ones such as the 1908 *Viscount* or the 1911 *Connaught*, and also appreciated a good turn of speed. He also sought out sea trips to Southend, Whitstable and elsewhere on board the *Princess Pocahontas* and was often to be seen on board *Waverley* during her annual visits to the area. Both his 70th and 80th birthday parties were held on board Thames passenger boats and, fittingly, his ashes were scattered into the river from *London Rose* during a final cruise.

Throughout his rich and varied life, Norman always kept his memories of sailing the Bristol Channel on board P. & A. Campbell's white funnelled paddle steamers especially close to his heart. It is therefore a great privilege to be able to share the following photographs of these much-loved ships and to pass on just a little of the delight he must have felt when taking them.

Richard Clammer

Norman Bird and friends on board Bristol Queen. L.to R. are Keith Abrahams, John Brown, Norman, Terry Cresswell (with camera), John Richardson and Ron Adams all of whom were enthusiastic members of the PSPS and Coastal Cruising Association, and sailed regularly on the Bristol Channel steamers. The photo may have been taken on board Bristol Queen during her first three-day excursion to the Scilly Isles in 1963.

Keith Adams collection

In the postwar period the appearance of *Ravenswood* was transformed. She had originally sported twin funnels when new in 1891. By the time she appeared in traffic operating the first postwar White Funnel excursions in 1946, she had been rebuilt and gained the modern style of 'concealed' paddle-boxes. She was the last P. & A. Campbell Ltd. paddle steamer in service with an open foredeck. She is seen here to perfection arriving off Penarth pier in 1951.

Ravenswood here is heading away from Penarth pier, on 8th June 1954. It was rare for her to stray far down Channel after WW2, and she appeared most frequently on the shorter up Channel sailings from Newport and Cardiff. She was withdrawn after the 'Centenary Year' of 1954. PSPS Bristol Channel branch members recall that she had become much slower towards the end of her life.

Now looking forlorn, **Ravenswood** went for scrapping at Cashmore's yard on the River Usk in Newport, after a period of lay-up in Bristol at the end of her career in the 1954 season. Her withdrawal was not immediate, as it had been intended to bring her out again for 1955, but she failed her survey, and was condemned accordingly. This photograph of her under tow was taken on 21st October 1955.

This photograph of **Ravenswood** after arrival at her final Newport resting place for breaking was also dated 21st October 1955. In his *Ship Ahoy* valedictory Norman Bird opined that after her withdrawal, every effort was made to operate the remaining four ships in the Bristol Channel as widely and imaginatively as possible, and the 1954 pattern of sailings was largely followed. Newport sailings were reduced, as were the less popular timings on the Bristol-Ilfracombe trips, and the Cardiff to Minehead afternoon trips were considerably fewer.

The one-time White Funnel Fleet flagship *Britannia* is here arriving off Weston super Mare on 10th June 1956, in what turned out to be her final season. When new in 1896, *Britannia* only had one funnel, and acquired this appearance following reconstruction after WW2, and reboilering. Her passengers could enjoy an abundance of open deck space.

Britannia is at anchor, off Lundy, on 15th July 1956. Enthusiasts knew by this time that she was in her final season, but by Norman Bird's account she was still a reliable member of the fleet, and possessed sufficient speed for the Lundy run from up Channel and reasonable time ashore on the island after landing on the beach by small boat.

Britannia at anchor off Lundy, on 22nd July 1955. Seen from the landing beach, her graceful lines can well be appreciated broadside on. There was little in the way of shelter on her promenade deck, but her accommodation on the main and lower decks basically remained as she had been after a very major 1930s makeover.

The final voyage of **Britannia**, under tow to the breakers, on 7th December 1956. In his writings in *Ship Ahoy*, the newsletter of the South Wales Branch of the World Ship Society, Norman Bird recognised the inevitability, as he put it, of the veteran members of the White Funnel Fleet being withdrawn as the 1950s progressed. But after this, when one third of the fleet had gone, (i.e. two paddlers out of six) it might have been hoped that there was yet still some future for the two ageing survivors and the modern pair, if deployed imaginatively.

Glen Usk was the third of a trio of mostly similar paddle steamers from the Ailsa shipbuilders, built between 1911 and 1914, and the only one to survive WW2 for further service. (The others were *Lady Ismay*, lost in WW1, and *Glen Avon*, lost in WW2). In the postwar years much o her time was spent on the Cardiff (Pier Head) to Weston super Mare "ferry" service, which often called at Penarth pier, where she was her photographed arriving during 1951. A general resemblance to *Britannia* may be detected, with abundant open deck space, but with slightl reduced diameter paddle wheels. She remained a coal burner to her end, although conversion to oil firing had been intended.

Possibly photographed on the same day as the previous image, **Glen Usk** is departing from Penarth in 1951, the location is identified by the distant view of the islands of Steep Holm and Flat Holm. This angle nicely shows the neat raised quarter-deck.

The founders of the Bristol company of P. & A. Campbell Ltd, which began operations in 1893 as a Limited Company, had Clyde roots, whic[ ] explains as well as can be the slightly odd nomenclature of some of the ships using the Scottish term *Glen* juxtaposed with an English c[ ] Welsh river. The 1914 built **Glen Usk** had been preceded in 1912 by the nearly identical **Glen Avon**. In earlier days there had been use c[ ] Scott literature for ship namings, with the first **Waverley** in 1885. This followed North British Railway ship nomenclature, in that the Clyd[ ] Campbell business acquired from them **Meg Merrilies** in 1885, and did not rename her, and then added a third ship to the Clyde fleet in 188[ ] **Madge Wildfire**. Subsequently **Ravenswood** continued this Scott theme, albeit for the company at Bristol. The paddle box detail of **Glen Us[ ]** is seen here in May 1958.

The setting of what was known colloquially – at least to local paddle steamer enthusiasts – at Cardiff as "The Drain", with Penarth Head rising up to the left, nicely shows a broadside profile of **Glen Usk**, dressed overall on this occasion, as she was due to encounter the Royal Yacht, on 3rd July 1957.

Glen Gower (b.1922) was the youngest of the quartet of pre-WW2 paddle steamers built for P. & A. Campbell Ltd which were to see furthe[r] service postwar. In common with the older ships, an abundance of open deck space was provided, in contrast to the postwar Queens whic[h] had generous deckhouse accommodation, like their near contemporary Clyde steamer *Waverley* (b.1947), which continues in the 21s[t] century in preservation. *Glen Gower* is seen going astern from Birnbeck Pier at Weston super Mare very late on in the season, on 7th Octobe[r] 1956. She had returned to the Bristol Channel having spent the main 1956 summer season at Brighton, up until the cessation of Campbe[ll] Sussex coast paddle steamer sailings that year, operated since around the beginning of the century.

Glen Gower is here arriving at Penarth in June 1952. She had a stately bearing, particularly when seen like this, and was a little larger than her Ailsa-built predecessors from 1911-1914. George Owen of Swansea, who as a small boy remembered seeing *Glen Gower* on her very first appearance at Swansea in June 1922, noted that she was an enlarged version of *Glen Usk*, being 11 ft. longer, fractionally wider, and deeper, with paddle wheels one foot greater in diameter, and eight floats on the wheel instead of seven.

Glen Gower is seen here alongside the unusually-shaped pier, almost three-sided, outside Ilfracombe Harbour early in the season, on 21s April 1954. After a short period in the Bristol Channel to get the 'Centenary Year' excursion sailings going at the commencement of the 195 season, *Glen Gower* left for Brighton to give sailings on the Sussex coast, and which included a limited resumption of cross-Channel sailing to France. She had performed this role for a few seasons in the inter-war years.

Although *Glen Gower* was withdrawn after the 1957 season, she lingered for a few years, her future undecided, before going to the breakers at Antwerp in 1960. Much of this period was spent in lay-up at Penarth Dock, where Norman Bird paid a visit on 5th March 1960, about a month before a tug arrived to tow her away.

ps BRISTOL QUEEN, 1946-1967

Despite the presence in the White Funnel Fleet from 1947 of the turbine steamer **Empress Queen**, built in 1940 but in need of reconstructio[n] after extensive wartime use, the paddle steamer **Bristol Queen** was built at Bristol, entered service in 1946, and took the role of flagship. Norman Bird travelled on board her when new, as a fourteeen year old schoolboy, but this was before his photographic career had begun. One of his earliest photographs of what had instantly become his favourite White Funnel Fleet paddle steamer was taken at Penarth in 1952. The twin funnelled ship had created a huge impression and it is easy to see why here. As well as her fine lines, many believed **Bristol Queen** had character and even personality, too.

Cardiff Queen was the second modern postwar paddle steamer to augment the White Funnel Fleet, and was Clyde-built like all of the prewar P. & A. Campbell Ltd. vessels. Both new ships had modern 'concealed' paddle boxes, and the Bristol built vessel was a little longer than her younger 'half-sister'. Whereas **Bristol Queen** was a one-off design, from the Charles Hill yard at Bristol, the design of **Cardiff Queen**, from the Clyde Fairfield yard, was based on the prewar Caledonian Steam Packet company pair of Clyde paddle steamers **Jupiter** and **Juno** built in 1937. In 1988 Nick James, a former Chairman of Waverley Steam Navigation authored the book *Cardiff Queen: The Ultimate Coastal Paddle Steamer*, the title of which cryptically gave a clue as towards why enthusiasts who knew both Queens intimately preferred one or the other, and could amicably argue over their respective merits and differences, and which was the better. Here, **Cardiff Queen** is off Weston-super-Mare on 16 July 1961, the first season in which the two Queens partnered one another after the four veterans had all been withdrawn.

Bristol Queen arriving at Bristol Hotwells seems the ideal place from which to set off through the spectacular Avon Gorge to begin a sort of clockwise circuit of the Bristol Channel by the paddle steamers of the postwar White Funnel Fleet, 31st May 1955.

On the same day **Bristol Queen** will have continued upstream, past the Hotwells pontoon berth to just beyond the entrance to the Cumberland Basin, there to swing, and then return the short distance back down river, to tie up at Hotwells for the next, outwards journey, 31st May 1955.

Norman Bird was distinctly of the opinion that the aft lifeboats on board **Bristol Queen** were an impediment to the enjoyment of coastal scenery, when they had originally been placed on deck in 1946 when new. By 1949, he recorded, the boats had been raised, but could still act as sails to an extent and hamper berthing in difficult winds. As can be seen, in this kind of dramatic steep sided location after setting off down the Avon Gorge from Bristol, the aft lifeboats in their davits retained an ungainly aspect, as seen here, on 20th May 1956.

Glen Usk is seen in the Avon Gorge, from almost the same vantage point as *Bristol Queen*, in her penultimate season, on 30th August 1959. Her aft lifeboat appears neatly suspended aloft when seen from this angle, compared to the much younger flagship.

Birnbeck Pier at Weston super Mare is about to see *Britannia* come alongside on 30th July 1956. South Walians such as Norman Bird could, on occasions, enjoy the option of sailing from Cardiff or Penarth to Weston super Mare on a 'ferry' crossing, and then change on to a down Channel sailing from Bristol to Ilfracombe, if no direct sailing from Cardiff to Ilfracombe was on offer that day. Prior to the closure of the Landing Stage at Newport after the 1956 season, and the enforced withdrawal of sailings from Newport, Newportonians similarly occasionally had the opportunity to change steamers at Weston's Birnbeck Pier.

This view of **Britannia** was also taken on 30th July 1956, whilst the ship was manoeuvring off Birnbeck Pier at Weston super Mare.

Still at Weston super Mare, **Ravenswood** appears to be working hard going astern, one day in 1953, either on an exceptionally lightly laden ferry crossing to Penarth and Cardiff, or possibly to Newport, or, as the tide is low, maybe to anchor off for a few hours to await the next flood. She is in Sand Bay here, with Sand Point (sometimes also referred to as Woodspring Point) visible in the left background.

Glen Gower is leaving Weston super Mare on 22nd May 1955, looking up-Channel, with Sand Bay to starboard. Like *Glen Usk*, she had a neatly-stowed aft lifeboat which caused no aesthetic offence. For much of the period when Norman Bird was photographically active, *Glen Gower* was the least accessible to Cardiffians of the Bristol Channel paddle steamers, as most of her seasons were spent either as the Swansea-based vessel, or away on the south coast, once referred to as "on the Brighton station".

Cardiff Queen at Weston super Mare on 8th August 1954. In the 1950s and particularly at weekends Cardiff and Newport visitors would arrive at Weston super Mare still in considerable numbers. Elaborate queuing arrangements on Birnbeck Island for passengers were necessary especially in the evenings to get everybody home safely, if there were multiple sailings to Penarth and Cardiff, as well as to Newport and to Bristol as well. Three or four vessels might have to use the single pier berth as quickly as possible in turn, with slick handling of multiple gangways vital, before the ebbing tide would halt operations. As well as those just arriving at Birnbeck Pier for the delights of Weston for the day, many South Walians also crossed to Weston in order to go on one of a range of P. & A. Campbell Ltd. inclusive coach tours, which ran from the pier gates, to places such as Cheddar Gorge, and Wells. All these coaches necessitated complex marshalling and crowd-handling.

A little way down the Somerset coast, **Cardiff Queen** is seen off Minehead on 4th October 1958. Minehead Pier did not survive WW2. When the steamers called at Minehead Harbour, which became available from 1951, the approach was generally made at this angle, with Bridgwater Bay in the distance behind, looking up Channel. The large Butlins Holiday Camp had yet to be built.

This sequence of four views on board *Cardiff Queen* was captured in May 1959, perhaps at the stage of a down Channel voyage after the Foreland has been passed, en route to Ilfracombe, perhaps from Cardiff, cruising along the spectacularly impressive north Devon coast. The white funnel was a striking sight.

Cardiff Queen, deck-view, looking forward, May 1959. She looks reasonably well patronised, and yet her attractive promenade deck space looks sufficiently spacious not to appear congested, on this occasion.

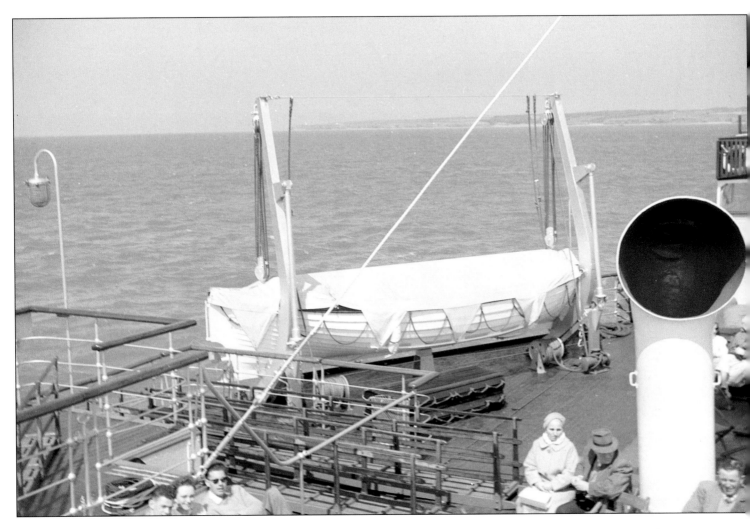

On board **Cardiff Queen**, detail of port sponson and forward lifeboat and davits, seen from atop the aft deckhouse, May 1959.

Many White Funnel Fleet passengers, Norman Bird reported, found the aft deck a particularly pleasing and indeed peaceful haven at sea, especially when returning up Channel, say to Penarth and Cardiff in the evening, maybe after a day in Devon, and when access was permitted. The deck had to be vacated prior to rope handling, maybe after rounding Lavernock Point on such a run. *Cardiff Queen*, May 1959.

Bristol Queen has slowed, or is almost stationary, off Lynmouth on 17th June 1954. She is crowded, and a small boat can just be seen pulling away from the rope ladder at the aft port sponson, with passengers destined for time ashore at Lynmouth. 1954 was designated 'Centenary Year', to commemorate 100 years since the beginning of the Campbell Clyde business at Kilmun, Holy Loch. A White Funnel Supporters Association had begun around then, some years before the PSPS was formed in 1959. After the Lynmouth flood disaster in August 1952 White Funnel steamer calls had only been reinstated in 1954, and so these could be promoted as a Centenary Year initiative, in marketing terms, as a happy coincidence.

Glen Usk occasionally had a little variety from the Cardiff-Weston 'ferry' duties with which she was associated so much in the 1950s. Late in the season, she is seen arriving at Ilfracombe, on 2nd October 1955, framed by Hillsborough Hill. The intrepid photographer had clambered over the side of the pier on to the rocks to line up this shot.

When approaching Ilfracombe from up Channel, Hele Bay is passed to port just moments before the paddler, in this case **Bristol Queen**, slows to pass the dramatic, steep Hillsborough Hill, and steers cautiously to take whichever berth is directed by the Ilfracombe Harbour Master, according to the state of the tide and any other movements in and out of the harbour. 18th September 1955.

Iso approaching Ilfracombe, and having glided past Hele Bay, **Cardiff Queen** also slows off Hillsborough and steers for her berth at the arbour. 2nd June 1954. Although a rope is about to be thrown from the forward starboard bow, there are still passengers right forward in the ow enjoying the experience of landfall at the north Devon harbour after a few hours at sea, in style and comfort, on a well found and still then tylish, modern paddle steamer, Campbell fashion.

This shot was described by Norman Bird as being of the farewell cruise of **Britannia**, at Ilfracombe, on 19th September 1956, and his memoir do not state what he did that day in order to have taken it. The schedule for **Britannia** was to depart Bristol 0845, Clevedon 0945, and arriv Ilfracombe 1250. The return departure from Ilfracombe was scheduled at 1600 to Clevedon (arr. 1910), with arrival back at Bristol at 2010, at special fare of two guineas, to include a fourchette luncheon and light tea. (Elsewhere, it was recorded that owing to the indisposition another fleet member, **Britannia** did make one or two more trips, before then definitively ceasing to run, after a remarkable sixty year career She truly enjoyed public affection, and perhaps especially so at Bristol, her home port of sixty years.

ne might reasonably deduce that Norman Bird travelled on **Britannia** down Channel to Ilfracombe for such an auspicious occasion, that of
er 'Farewell Cruise' on 19th September 1956, took the preceding picture, and enjoyed the atmosphere ashore for an hour or two. He then
ter strolled around the harbour to capture this view of **Britannia** returning from the anchorage, then hurried back for the return voyage to
ristol. The old pier (then newly reconstructed) is clearly seen here to advantage from Larkstone.

A favourite spot in Ilfracombe for visitors used to be Rapparee Cove, once reachable by a short ferry journey across the harbour. After a walk right around the inner harbour, it was also a good place to photograph the classic scene of a Campbell steamer alongside the pier outside the outer harbour, nestling underneath Lantern Hill. On this occasion *Glen Gower* is the steamer at rest on 2nd October 1955, framed by Rapparee Cove, albeit devoid of pleasure seekers this late in the year.

Glen Gower alongside the outermost portion of Ilfracombe pier may well have arrived earlier than Norman Bird (i.e. by a different steamer from up Channel) on 28 July 1952, as she was stationed at Swansea for much of the 1952 season. There were still occasions when multiple White Funnel steamers might be together at Ilfracombe, perhaps as many as four on some days in that year, if one came from each of Bristol, Newport, Cardiff and Swansea.

Seen from Ilfracombe Harbour, and described by Norman Bird as leaving for the last time, *Glen Gower*, 29th September 1957. She ha
evidently become less reliable as the 1957 season progressed, the finances of P. & A. Campbell Ltd. were still troublesome after the majc
cutbacks of 1956, and so she was put aside. That left just the two modern ships to continue for 1958, supported by a third paddler *Glen Us*
for the Cardiff-Weston 'ferry', Newport sailings having ceased after 1956.

Glen Usk is seen alongside at Ilfracombe Harbour a few years earlier, in better times, on 2nd October 1954. This was towards the end of the Centenary Year, when the White Funnel Fleet of paddle steamers remained six strong, but would begin to contract thereafter.

Cardiff Queen: serenity prevails, and no crew-member is to be seen as the Clyde built paddler rests off Ilfracombe on 15th June 1958. This picture looks very like it was taken from the Tunnels beach, one afternoon, during time ashore, on a pleasant day. Around that time Norman Bird had made his first visit to the Clyde, and was suitably impressed with the great variety of excursion steamers, but nevertheless concluded that personally he preferred the Bristol Channel, for its diversity of sailing opportunities, and of course ***Bristol Queen***.

A pair of Queens, as **Cardiff Queen** is framed off Ilfracombe by the lifeboat of **Bristol Queen**, on 12th August 1956. The ticket office on the younger vessel was located almost under the bridge, in a transverse passageway open either side, such that a newly purchased ticket might easily blow away in the wind if not held securely!

Occasional sailings to Bideford were re-introduced in 1954. This sailing on Saturday 2nd July 1955, was advertised to depart from Ilfracombe at 1400 for Bideford. The return time from Bideford was at 1730 via Ilfracombe, the ship then continuing to Swansea. Norman Bird probably sailed down Channel from Cardiff that morning to do the Bideford trip on **Cardiff Queen**, which gave brief time ashore there, whilst the vessel carried out a short, Torridge river cruise from Bideford, on which she has here just departed, outward-bound towards the Bar.

Cardiff Queen is seen again on Saturday 2nd July 1955 on the Torridge cruise outwards from Bideford. Norman Bird probably changed ships at Ilfracombe after returning there (i.e. on *Cardiff Queen*) in order to return up Channel to Cardiff on a different vessel. This must surely have been the ideal Bristol Channel full day out, with the beauty and novelty of the Torridge river and estuary as well as the delight, to a by now hardened enthusiast, of changing steamers at 'Combe, which had been a much more common practice before the war.

Another of the occasional White Funnel Fleet paddle steamer trips to the River Torridge was that undertaken on 5th August 1956 by **Bristol Queen**, framed here by the tree lined Bideford Quay.

The promenade deck of **Glen Gower** is worryingly quiet on a calm evening, in May 1957, in what turned out to be her final season in Bristol Channel service. It could of course have been biting cold, making dining or drinking down below a more appealing alternative part of the ship to be in. Donald Anderson, a close associate of Norman Bird, and Editor of *Ship Ahoy* in 1957, (and later the energetic PSPS Bristol Channel Branch former Chairman), pithily wrote about the final year of **Glen Gower** largely spent on 'ferry' duties, after the abolition of restaurant facilities, when '*the dining saloon has been converted into a bar, which successfully absorbs the inebriates who inevitably spoil the last trip from Weston on Sunday evening*'.

Clovelly, just a few miles further down the north Devon coast, was visited by White Funnel Fleet steamers from Ilfracombe somewhat more frequently than Bideford could be. No tidal limitations applied at Clovelly. **Britannia** was the means by which Norman Bird enjoyed a long day out on Tuesday 19th July 1955 from Cardiff, which was advertised to begin at 0915, and call at Penarth Pier, and also at Barry Pier en-route to Ilfracombe. The return departure time from Clovelly was advertised at 1600. Small boats brought passengers ashore to the beach.

Passengers may have been able to enjoy a couple of hours ashore at Clovelly if they had come all the way from the up-Channel piers, depending on numbers, how many local boatmen were mustered to ferry them, at twelve per boat, and of course weather conditions. *Britannia* here is seen from the War Memorial, again on Tuesday 19th July 1955. The same ship had run excursions such as this, requiring her good speed, from the up-Channel ports to Clovelly, from when she was new in 1896. The harbour wall can just about be made out, far below the folk sat at ease.

Bristol Queen is seen at Clovelly in Centenary Year, on 16th June 1954, when calls were reintroduced at the furthermost White Funnel Flee calling point in Devon. Clovelly offered paddler passengers a great welcome, whether for a cream tea, Devon cider, pasties, or just the superlative views and its general picturesqueness.

Bristol Queen is again seen at Clovelly, on 16th June 1954. Surely no excuse is needed for the generous photographic coverage Norman Bird gave to such a delightful destination as the perfect combination of scenery and steamer at rest.

Bristol Queen is yet again seen at Clovelly, but this time on 16th July 1956, and with a good view looking up the Bristol Channel across Bideford Bay, and with traditional boating of ferry passengers using enterprising muscle power.

final look at *Bristol Queen* off Clovelly, a couple of years later, on 26th May 1958, and after the strength of the postwar White Funnel Fleet
ad contracted from six paddle steamers to just three, but would further reduce to two. In this view Lundy is out of sight, yet not far distant
om Clovelly.

Lundy in 1955. **Britannia** lies serenely at anchor in the landing bay on the east coast of the island on 22nd July 1955, with Rat Island seen a fairly low tide, and so looking just about joined to the main part of the island. The landing beach is not quite in sight in this view from the roa which ascends from the bay to Millcombe, then the owner's residence. A little higher up above Millcombe lies the Marisco Tavern, just a welcoming to **Waverley** passengers nowadays as to those arriving the same way on **Britannia** back then.

Before ascending to the summit of the island there came the voyage ashore by one of the launches kept at Lundy by P. & A. Campbell Ltd. for the purpose. **Bristol Queen** has arrived at the island, here, on 20 September 1955. The fare, to land, either single or day-return, in 1955 was thirteen shillings and sixpence, 'Weather and Circumstances Permitting', as the handbills put it. The passage from Ilfracombe took about an hour and a half. In those days Campbell sailings from Ilfracombe may have been offered at least two or three times weekly. Norman Bird confessed to being smitten with Lundy, and many still are, however they get to the Atlantic island.

Cardiff Queen off Lundy, 4th August 1959.

Bristol Queen off Lundy, 23rd May 1961. Lundy was private property then, yet most welcoming. P. & A. Campbell Ltd kept their own launches on the island, by agreement with the then owners the Harman family.

Back from Lundy to the Devon mainland, and **Cardiff Queen** lies off the beach at Clovelly on 7th June 1960. When there were more steamers in the fleet, particularly when one was still stationed at Swansea, it was not uncommon for there to be sailings from Ilfracombe to Lundy via Clovelly, giving intrepid Clovelly holidaymakers the option of four small-boat voyages in one day-excursion, on and off the steamer at either place. The practice had ceased by this time, but Clovelly remained a White Funnel destination into the 1970s, with willing boatmen who were still prepared to handle smaller numbers maybe only weekly.

rather different take on the Clovelly scene, where the detail of the shore handling of waiting passengers interested the photographer ufficiently to dominate over the more distant stern view of *Cardiff Queen* on 5th August 1965. At this time the newest White Funnel Fleet addle steamer was approaching the end of her days, but this was not known then, and trading in the early 1960s with just the pair of modern eamers had outwardly appeared to be viable. Late in the season of 1965 a third ship, the fairly elderly motor-vessel *Vecta* from the Isle of /ight, joined the Bristol Channel fleet. This former ferry would later be renamed *Westward Ho*, and effectively take the place of a paddle eamer, but there was to be a three-strong White Funnel Fleet in 1966.

Bristol Queen at Padstow, north Cornwall, on 8th August 1965. This was a Paddle Steamer Preservation Society charter, and the first call at Padstow by a Campbell vessel since 1938. Padstow was 'en fete' for the occasion, as Norman Bird put it, and the trip was highly successful having begun at Swansea, with a bus connection from Cardiff. The success of the trip induced the company to repeat it themselves in 1966 and 1967 on a few occasions.

ristol Queen at Padstow on 8th August 1965, the numbers of people demonstrating the popularity of this destination, rather beyond the ⌐nits of what is generally thought of as the Bristol Channel, but a delightful 3 or 4-hour sea voyage from Ilfracombe, round Hartland Point, and ᴐwn the Cornish coast, to rendezvous with the obligatory pilot, to proceed up the River Camel.

Another trip was taken by Norman Bird to Padstow a year later, again on **Bristol Queen**, on 28th July 1966. Even back then, it was recognised amongst the paddle steamer enthusiast fraternity that it was commendably enterprising on the part of Campbell's management, in view of the great distance steamed, and thus the larger fuel bills than on a normal day. Added to this, there was risk of weather disruption, and delays, with only a fairly narrow tidal window to navigate up the tidal River Camel.

As with the occasional Bideford trips when a short Torridge river cruise out of that port was offered, **Bristol Queen** on 28th July 1966 also offered a short cruise for local residents out of Padstow down the Camel river to view the coast. Already a lovely Cornish coastal scene the rapidly disappearing elegant stern of the departing paddle steamer could only enhance the scene further, especially to a White Funnel devotee.

The clockwise tour continues, in a manner of speaking, by now crossing the mouth of the outermost Bristol Channel, from north Devon to Pembrokeshire in west Wales. Norman Bird recorded that the first postwar visit by a Campbell steamer to Milford Haven took place in 1955. He had crossed on **Bristol Queen** from Milford Haven and Tenby to Ilfracombe on 17 April 1961, the occasion of her first call there. This was after two years absence of the ship when laid up for the 1959 and 1960 seasons, and it was 'sheer heaven' to be back on board his favourite ship on such a trip. This picture was taken on 30th August 1964, described by him as the annual Milford Haven trip (until 1967).

Compared to the rarity of far-distant Milford Haven, Tenby in west Wales was visited occasionally in the 1950s, often by the Swansea-based steamer until the closure of the "Swansea station" after the 1958 Season. Tenby's promenade pier might have vanished, but the harbour remained accessible, and **Cardiff Queen** visited the truly charming little Pembrokeshire port, as seen here on 17th July 1955.

Bristol Queen at Tenby on 12th August 1954. Norman Bird recorded this as the first visit of the Bristol built paddler to the Pembrokeshir harbour. Before WW2 Tenby was sometimes the destination of a day excursion by paddle steamer from Ilfracombe.

ristol Queen at Tenby, also pictured on 12th August 1954. Not long before this view was taken, demolition of the remains of the old pier which ran out from the headland near the lifeboat station slipway had been completed. The Tenby Royal Victoria pier dated from the 1890s, nd was one of the later Bristol Channel piers to be built, and had been used by Campbell paddlers before WW2.

Bristol Queen at Mumbles on 30th May 1966, although this is not entirely obvious unless one has stood on the pier and looked across Swansea Bay on a lovely clear day, and gazed at industrial Port Talbot on the horizon. It took many years for Mumbles Pier to be reopened to steamers after WW2, in 1956 eventually, very soon after which the withdrawal of the Swansea based steamer left it very lightly served. In common with Clovelly on the English side, Mumbles Pier was still a most attractive destination on the Welsh side of the Bristol Channel in Campbell's later years and the White Funnel Fleet was down to just one ship, mv ***Balmoral***.

Visits by **Bristol Queen** to Swansea were rare in the 1950s, but more common in the 1960s when Norman Bird recorded that the two surviving modern paddlers interchanged duties. From 1961 one or the other would often spend days on the Cardiff to Weston 'ferry', rather ignominiously, he felt, for steamers better suited to long distance cruising. This view dates from 8th August 1965, the vessel alongside **Bristol Queen** at Swansea Pockett's Wharf is the local pilot boat, **Seamark**. The camera was pointing out to sea in this view of the River Tawe, with the larger part of Swansea Docks to the left side of the picture. South Dock lay to the right.

A slightly unusual occurrence in the 1954 'Centenary Year' was when two steamers were at Swansea on the same day, for this photograph of **Cardiff Queen** was described as being of her leaving Swansea for Ilfracombe, and dated 4th September 1954.

Taken on the same day, on 4th September 1954, this view of **Cardiff Queen** was described as being of her leaving Swansea for a cruise, seen from on board **Glen Usk**. Norman Bird wrote about occasional breakdowns of the more modern ship, which was often the Swansea based vessel, and which were attributed to boiler mounting problems occurring when she lay overnight on the Pockett's Wharf mud berth on the River Tawe, close to the city centre of Swansea. These were eventually traced and rectified, and this picture may have been taken on an occasion when **Glen Usk** was to have a spell at Swansea in lieu of 'CQ'. The fleet was still six strong in 1954.

Glen Usk enters Swansea on 4th September 1954.

Glen Usk is swinging in the mouth of the Tawe at Swansea, on 4th September 1954. The P. & A. Campbell Ltd. presence on 'the Swansea station' only dated from 1920, and there had been a number of seasons in which *Glen Usk* had been the regular Swansea steamer in her younger days. Right up until the end of the Swansea steamer in the 1958 season, it was still usual to provide a couple of Swansea-Ilfracombe return crossings on Summer Saturdays. The quaint phrase 'luggage passengers' might still be used, when this popular service for Devon bound holidaymakers was provided as well as for day excursionists. Norman Bird noted that it became more operationally challenging to continue to give Saturday Swansea to Ilfracombe crossings when only two ships were left in the Bristol Channel, and which covered Cardiff, Bristol and the 'ferry', yet by working long hours and with clever timetabling Campbell's still provided a service.

Cardiff Queen is about to ease off before arriving at Porthcawl harbour, on 15th June 1958. This was during the last year of the Swansea based steamer, and calls at Porthcawl became less frequent afterwards.

Cardiff Queen is pictured departing from Porthcawl harbour on 15th June 1958.

The clockwise tour of the piers and harbours of the Bristol Channel, as visited by Norman Bird mostly in the 1950s and early 1960s, and which began at Bristol and thence proceeded down the English side, nears its end as we continue to head back up the Welsh side along the Glamorgan coast. There was once a great rival to the then mighty Campbell White Funnel Fleet, in the form of the Red Funnel Line. This competing fleet was based at Barry, where the Barry Railway Company opened their own pier in 1899. One of the very earliest pictures Norman Bird took was this superbly detailed view of the unusual rail connected Barry Pier, with the oldest member of the prewar White Funnel Fleet quartet *Ravenswood* in attendance, in 1949. The pier was available for steamer calls at all states of the tide.

Although dating from 1896 *Britannia* underwent reboilering after WW2, and looked spruce with a new pair of funnels. Here *Britannia* approaches Penarth pier in 1949, looking up Channel towards Newport. She may well have been destined for Ilfracombe, or equally plying between Cardiff and Weston, or on a run to Bristol.

Glen Usk has just eased away from Penarth Pier in April 1952. The pier at Penarth opened in 1895. The amount of shipping that passed Penarth Pier heading to or from Cardiff Docks, just round the corner, impressed the youthful Norman Bird greatly before WW2, when taken there by his parents on outings from Cardiff where the family lived. Penarth Pier looks remarkably similar nowadays when the preserved paddle steamer ***Waverley*** makes use of it on annual but all too brief visits away from the Clyde to the Bristol Channel. The Pier Head facilities at Cardiff lapsed out of use as long ago as 1971, and long before the development of Cardiff Bay, so Penarth Pier has been the main point of embarkation for ***Waverley*** excursions in south Wales for over forty years now.

Glen Gower is seen here in the 'Drain' from off Penarth Head (right background), with Cardiff Docks to the left of picture, on 17th July 1957. She appears to be arriving, and is very close to the pair of pontoons where four steamers could berth, one each side of either structure. There was little margin for error, steering-wise, or with rope-handling, in the confined space, and especially when the tide was ebbing rapidly. Norman Bird was in no doubt that it demanded great skill to berth safely at Cardiff, but equally noted there were rarely any incidents, by experienced crews.

The small boat off the aft starboard quarter of *Glen Gower* requires explanation: to assist a quick turn round of the steamer at the Cardiff Pier Head berth, a rope would be passed to the boatman as the steamer slowed right down, which was then taken to the quay wall near the Dock Offices. This rope was then fastened around a bollard ashore. Once secured like this, the steamer having made fast on the pontoon berth, when ready to leave, the stern winch would be used to pull on this rope until the vessel was pointing back down the 'Drain' to proceed out to sea. In Norman Bird's time in the 1950s, and to a lesser extent in the 1960s after fleet cutbacks, Cardiff was the place where the greatest numbers of White Funnel passengers were handled, and equally was usually the only place where two or occasionally more steamers overnighted. It was also the place where the three coal burning steamers bunkered, apart from being a location of immense character.

Rounding off our clockwise, postwar White Funnel Fleet tour of the Bristol Channel, and having failed to illustrate a paddle steamer up the River Usk alongside the pontoon berth at Newport, opposite the remains of the castle, we instead end up not on a paddle steamer at all. Here we are looking over the poop deck of the then relatively recently acquired motor vessel *Westward Ho*, way upstream in the Severn estuary on Saturday 30 April 1966. This was a sailing very like those occasionally still operated in the 21st century by ps *Waverley*, but which commenced at Cardiff Pier Head, (*now gone*), then proceeded via Penarth Pier, (*happily extant*), crossed the channel to Weston Birnbeck Pier (*sadly now almost a complete ruin*), and then continued on to Clevedon Pier, still intact in 1966 before its famous collapse (*but nowadays lovingly restored and, like Penarth, happily still extant, and available for steamer calls*), for an Up The Severn cruise.

Construction of the Severn Bridge had got underway in 1963, and Norman Bird wrote that his beloved *Bristol Queen* undertook her last sailing of the season and conveyed around 1,000 passengers to view the official opening of the Severn Bridge by H.M. the Queen on 0⁸ September 1966. On the following day *Bristol Queen* entered the dock at Cardiff to lay up for the Winter. *Cardiff Queen* continued in service until 21 September 1966, and shortly afterwards was put up for sale. The motor vessel *Westward Ho* remained in the White Funnel Fleet after the tragic major breakdown of *Bristol Queen* in 1967, and her instant withdrawal. The smaller motor vessel *St. Trillo* was recalled from north Wales to help out in the Bristol Channel in late 1967, and again in 1968, and Campbell services generally were further assisted for periods in the late 1960s by the chartering in of *Queen of the Isles*, a spare ship from the Isles of Scilly. *Balmoral* joined *Westward Ho* from 1969, but after the latter expired in 1971 the former was left on her own for the next few years.

This is roughly the top third of a typical, double sided handbill, (*reduced in size here*) of nearly A3 size, advertising the excursions of the White Funnel Fleet of P. & A. Campbell Ltd. for the early season of 1966. The fleet listed here requires some clarification, as only the first four ships named underneath the header comprised the excursion fleet in 1966. The other four vessels named were launches, the first three having been given the names of earlier Campbell paddlers, namely *Ravenswood* (b. 1891), *Waverley* (b.1907, originally named *Barry*), and *Devonia* (b. 1905), the latter pair having been built for the Barry Railway Company. *Lundy Queen* was clearly deemed a nice name for a Lundy launch, or at least in keeping with the postwar White Funnel Fleet image.

On the well used bill which covered the 1966 early season sailings from Cardiff, Penarth and Barry Piers, this was the entry for the day on which Norman Bird voyaged up Channel, as a change from going down Channel. This was to view the new Severn Bridge, on board mv *Westward Ho*, on Saturday 30 April 1966. (She had been renamed from her former Isle of Wight name of *Vecta* after the brief appearance in the Campbell fleet in late 1965, and undergone attention during the winter of 1965-1966). As can be gleaned from studying each of the excursion opportunities on offer that day, all handled by the single ship, there was no water at Cardiff at breakfast time so a train was provided to enable Cardiff passengers to join the ship at Barry Pier where it was afloat. Equally, the schedule for mv *Westward Ho* ended that day at Barry Pier.

WHITE FUNNEL FLEET

BRISTOL QUEEN   CARDIFF QUEEN   WESTWARD HO   ST. TRILLO   RAVENSWOOD   WAVERLEY   DEVONIA   LUNDY QUEEN

Sailings from

CARDIFF (Pier Head) PENARTH & BARRY PIERS

The Westward Ho which will be operating the services during the period advertised on this leaflet, is a motor vessel of 630 tons. The vessel has a cafeteria, tea lounge, bars also spacious open decks and covered accommodation is available for all passengers.

April 7th — May 15th, 1966

B.P. and to B.P.—Times from and to Barry Pier.
†—These steamers sail direct to Cardiff and call at Penarth on the next outward journey.
★—These steamers do not call at Penarth.
⊂—Book at Cardiff (Gen.) for these trips, or on board Steamers, passengers may join or leave trains at intermediate stations.
All Weston steamers call at Penarth 10 minutes later than Cardiff, except where otherwise shown.

SPECIAL FACILITIES FOR PASSENGERS EMBARKING AT BARRY
When a sailing is advertised from Barry to Weston and the only return steamer from Weston is to Penarth and Cardiff and not to Barry, Passengers who embark at Barry and purchase their tickets on the steamer may, if they desire, disembark at Penarth and travel by free bus to Barry (Town Hall). The last bus from Penarth to Barry (Town Hall) leaves at 10.30 p.m.

2 HOUR CRUISES IN THE CHANNEL—FARE 8/6d.
On days where trips are advertised as "2 Hour Cruises in the Channel", the steamer from Weston is to Penarth and Cardiff and back across the Channel to Weston, then back to Cardiff and Penarth. The times of departures are given below together with the fare applicable to each trip. The total journey occupies approximately 2 hours or a little over. Passengers holding cheap cruise tickets will not be able to land at Weston.

THURSDAY, APRIL 7th
WESTON. Leave Cardiff 8.50, 11.0 a.m. (BP 5.15 p.m.). Leave Weston

WEDNESDAY, APRIL 13th
WESTON. Leave Cardiff 9.20, 11.30 a.m., 3.50 p.m. Leave Weston †10.30 a.m., †2.45, 8.20 p.m.
2 HOUR CRUISE IN THE CHANNEL. Leave Cardiff 9.20 a.m., Penarth 9.30 a.m.
Afternoon trip to WESTON. Leave Cardiff 3.50 p.m., Penarth 4.0 p.m. Leave Weston 8.20 p.m. for Penarth and Cardiff. Fare 13/6d.
THURSDAY, APRIL 14th
WESTON. Leave Cardiff 10.0 a.m., 2.0, 5.30 p.m. Leave Weston 11.10 a.m., †4.30 p.m. (7.0 p.m. to BP).
On this day passengers may return from Weston at 7.0 p.m. to Barry Pier and be issued with a free rail ticket to Cardiff, if they so desire.
2 HOUR CRUISE IN THE CHANNEL. Leave Cardiff 10.0 a.m., Penarth 10.10 a.m.
Afternoon trip to WESTON and Cruise around the STEEP HOLM ISLAND. Leave Cardiff 2.0 p.m., Penarth 2.10 p.m. Leave Weston 4.30 p.m. for Cardiff and Penarth or leave Weston 7.0 p.m. for Barry Pier and free rail to Cardiff. Fare 13/6d. Including Cruise 15/6d.
Evening Cruise calling at WESTON PIER and returning to Barry Pier and free rail to Cardiff. Leave Cardiff 5.30 p.m., Penarth 5.40 p.m., back Barry 8.0 p.m. Fare 9/6d.
FRIDAY, APRIL 15th
NO SAILINGS THIS DAY
SATURDAY, APRIL 16th
WESTON. Leave Cardiff 2.0, 4.15 p.m. Leave Weston †3.10, †5.30 p.m.
⊂Single trip to ILFRACOMBE via Barry Pier. Connecting train leaves Cardiff (General) 6.41 a.m. Steamer leaves Barry Pier 7.10 a.m., due to arrive Ilfracombe 9.55 a.m. Inclusive fare (Rail and Steamer) 27/6d.
**⊂Morning Cruise calling at ILFRACOMBE and returning to Penarth and

---

SATURDAY, APRIL 30th
WESTON. Leave Cardiff 12.40, 6.45 p.m. (BP 10.35 a.m.). Leave Weston †11.40 a.m., †5.40 p.m. (8.0 p.m. to BP).
On this day passengers may return from Weston to Barry at 8.0 p.m. and be issued with a free rail ticket to Cardiff, if they so desire.
¶Day trip to WESTON via Barry Pier. Connecting train leaves Cardiff (General) 9.41 a.m. Steamer leaves Barry Pier 10.35 a.m. Leave Weston 11.40 a.m. or 5.40 p.m. for Cardiff and Penarth only or 8.0 p.m. for Barry Pier and train to Cardiff. Inclusive return fare (Rail and Steamer) 17/6d.
Day trip to WESTON from Barry. Leave Barry 10.35 a.m. Leave Weston 8.0 p.m. for Barry.
Afternoon trip to WESTON, CLEVEDON and Cruise up the RIVER SEVERN to view the New Severn Bridge. Leave Cardiff 12.40 p.m., Penarth 12.50 p.m., due to arrive Clevedon 2.30 p.m. Leave Clevedon 4.50 p.m., Weston 5.40 p.m. for Cardiff and Penarth or leave Weston 8.0 p.m. for Barry Pier and free rail to Cardiff. Fares: Weston or Clevedon 15/-, to include Cruise 16/-.
Evening Cruise calling at WESTON PIER and returning to Barry Pier and free rail to Cardiff. Leave Cardiff 6.45 p.m., Penarth 6.55 p.m., back Barry 9.0 p.m. Fare 9/6d.

As a diversion from capturing beautiful ships in great settings and applying considerable compositional skills, Norman Bird also somehow managed to capture the atmosphere on board the White Funnel Fleet of paddle steamers, with their impressive sense of space which gave that serenity at sea that he wrote about so fluently. Towards the end of the life of the Ailsa built *Glen Usk* dating back 1914, and then the oldest survivor when seen here on 02 May 1959, the first of this quartet of pictures records the promenade deck, looking forward along the starboard side.

Taken almost from the bow, on a very quiet crossing, here is the open bridge atop the chart room of *Glen Usk*, for the hardy captain & steersman.

With a roll film camera in the 1950s, the engine room alleyway of **Glen Usk** was photographically more challenging than an on deck shot. The more enclosed character of the engine room panelling dividing it off from the main deck is quite different to **Waverley**, seen here on 02 May 1959. If one stuck one's head inside (the door was invariably left open, and the Chief Engineer was usually remembered as friendly), there was a rewarding spectacle of whizzing cranks.

By the late 1950s, full restaurant service had long ceased on board **Glen Usk**, and snacks could be obtained from a counter at the stern of this area, then best described as the 'buffet lounge', on the main deck, aft. PSPS Bristol Channel Branch members whose memories stretch back to the 1950s refer to the forward main deck area on **Glen Usk**, with sparred seating, as often being occupied by off duty stokers, on the last Campbell coal burner. The bar on **Glen Usk** was below the main deck (like the one on **Waverley**, but forward rather than aft) but there were no liquid refreshments available elsewhere. 02 May 1959.

After the end of the 1962 season it was arranged that **Bristol Queen** was in need of an extensive overhaul. P. & A. Campbell Ltd. had closed down their own Bristol workshop and maintenance facility after the 1956 season, and so the specialist attention of Cosens & Co. Ltd. of Weymouth, still then running their vintage paddle steamers on the Dorset coast, was engaged. She left Cardiff on 12 November 1962 and had an excellent voyage around Land's End without incurring delay. Our photographer journeyed there to photograph her, on 19 January 1963, and found her tucked away and in company with Cosen's own **Embassy**. It was not until 27 April 1963 that **Bristol Queen** returned to Cardiff after delays caused by bad weather, but some measure of the extensive work undertaken can be understood from the stay of months rather than weeks.

The return of **Bristol Queen** to front-line service in 1963 was hugely welcomed by enthusiasts, and it would then have seemed that she had a positive and secure future after such investment. The first foray by **Bristol Queen** to the Isles of Scilly went off with aplomb in May 1963, was portrayed at the beginning of this pictorial anthology. On a more negative note **Glen Usk** was towed away from Cardiff to ship-breakers at Passage West in Ireland on the evening tide of Monday 29 April 1963.

orman Bird was joint-editor of *Ship Ahoy* with Donald Anderson in the early 1960s, and in the Summer 1963 edition he wrote a full account ntitled "An Historic Occasion", which concisely documented the first trip made by his beloved ***Bristol Queen*** from Cardiff to Penzance and e Isles of Scilly, over the weekend Friday 17 May to Sunday 19 May 1963. He paid tribute to the management of P. & A. Campbell Ltd. who ook over' the trip from a would be charterer who ran into financial difficulties. The PSPS had been involved in ticket sales, and Mr. Smith-Cox, e Managing Director, arranged for the trip to go ahead. A special class 2 certificate was arranged, and the maximum capacity permitted was st 144 passengers. With 41 crew, this combined to the maximum lifeboat capacity of 185. This shot, captured on the paddle box of ***Bristol ueen*** at Penzance before departure at 1045 on Saturday 18 May, shows Captain George (with his back to the camera), Mr. Smith-Cox (in lby), Chief Officer Philip Power, and the local Penzance pilot. It was recorded that 120 passengers enjoyed the special excursion, that the eather was clement, and the ship was back on time on the Sunday night.

Performing on board a cruise out of Cardiff on board *Bristol Queen* one evening in July 1956, the excitement and atmosphere generated by Shirley Bassey is palpable.

About the PSPS

The Paddle Steamer Preservation Society (PSPS) is Britain's largest and most successful steamship preservation group with around 2500 members. Since its formation in 1959, the PSPS has saved two historic paddle steamers – PS Waverley and PS Kingswear Castle – both in service in the UK.

The PSPS has provided over £3.8 million to ensure Waverley continues to sail, making the Society the single largest Waverley supporter group. The PSPS has also provided over £600,000 to enable works on Kingswear Castle to ensure her future. As a charity, the PSPS welcomes bequests and legacies. We invite you to join us and play your part to help keep both ships sailing.

Benefits of PSPS Membership

- Support for Waverley & Kingswear Castle
- 2 Free Waverley tickets for children each year
- Free full colour A4 "Paddle Wheels" magazine every 3 months
- Access discounted Waverley Cruising Vouchers
- Regular meetings across the UK
- Enjoy your next Waverley cruise at half price when you join PSPS aboard Waverley

Full details of all membership benefits from our website at paddlesteamers.org/join

The Paddle Steamer Preservation Society is a Company limited by Guarantee No. 2167853 (England & Wales. It is a Charity registered in England & Wales (298328) and in Scotland (SC037603). Registered Office: Mayfield, Hoe Lane, Abinger Hammer, Dorking RH5 6RS.

Aims of the PSPS

- To preserve Paddle Steamers in operation in the UK
- To communicate the historic significance of Paddle Steamers in the Nation's maritime and industrial heritage
- To acquire, preserve and exhibit a collection of equipment and material associated with Paddle Steamers

The PSPS Collection

The PSPS Collection continues to expand with over 50,000 items. This is the largest collection of materials relating to Paddle Steamers including postcards, sailing bills, books, souvenirs and fittings from much loved steamers of the past. We welcome further donations to enhance our collection.

Paddle Wheels

Each issue of the magazine gives the latest news on Waverley and Kingswear Castle, as well as regular updates on Maid of the Loch and Medway Queen. Also included are articles on steamers of the past, items in our collection, and local Branch meetings.

Social Media Channels

With regular updates on the Society and our ships

 paddlesteamers   🐦 @PSPS_UK

 PSPS Scottish Branch   📷 psps_uk

Contact PSPS

membership@paddlesteamers.org

38 Merrylee Park Avenue, Giffnock, Glasgow G46 6HR